Waffle weave crochet is a stitch that forms a thick, stretchy, interlocking double layer of fabric.

The interlocking of two layers produces a dimpled surface that looks like a waffle iron imprint. The dimples trap air into little pockets which creates a fabric that is very warm. It is the air pockets, not the tightness, thickness, or weight of the yarn/crochet, that contribute to the warmth.

The right side of the fabric shows on both front and back. This makes pieces reversible.

Gauge

Obtaining an accurate gauge is difficult in this stitch because the stitch is so stretchy and the interlocking causes the fabric to shrink in over the first few rows. Make a large swatch and measure the gauge near the top. If you are part way through a project and find your gauge is off slightly, even though you made a swatch and are working to the swatch specifications, you will probably be OK because the fabric is so stretchy.

Pattern Notes

You work through the front loops when making the waffle weave stitch. Front and back loops are named from the side of the crochet facing you -- when you turn your work, what was a front loop becomes a back loop and vice versa!

The front of the fabric is the side facing you at the moment. The back of the fabric is the side away from you at the moment. These change when you turn your work!

The right side of the fabric is the side that is the good side or outside when a project is completed. The wrong side of the fabric is the bad side, back side, or inside.

The Stitch

The waffle weave stitch is worked back and forth (i.e. with turns) even when working in the round as for a hat. Use a knife (palm) grip to reduce hand fatigue. Switch to the knife grip even if you use a pencil grip for your other crochet.

You will be using hooks that may seem too large for the yarn weight. However, smaller hooks cause the fabric to be stiff and reduce the size of the air pockets so the fabric is not as warm.

To learn the waf ... 14 chs.

Row 1: Sk first ch, sc in front lp (*see Photo A*) of each rem ch, turn.

Front loops of beg ch

Photo A

Row 2: Ch 1, *insert hook from bottom to top under front lp of beg ch (this was the back bump of beg ch that was not used in row 1; it became the front lp when you turned your work), insert hook from bottom to top under front lp of sc of row 1 directly above ch, yo, draw through 2 front lps, yo and draw through 2 lps on hook; rep from * across, turn.

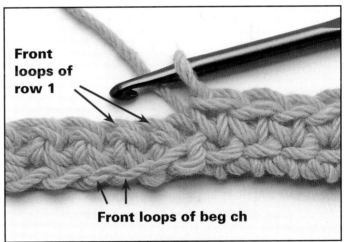

Front loops of row 1

Front loops of beg ch

Photo B

In the project instructions, this is written (sc tog front lp of beg ch and row 1) across, turn.

Row 3: Ch 1, *insert hook from bottom to top under front lp of sc in row 1 (two rows previous, the front lps form a horizontal line across the bottom of the piece), insert hook from bottom to top under front lp of sc in row 2 (previous row), (yo, draw through 2 front lps, yo and draw through 2 lps on hook; rep from * across, turn.

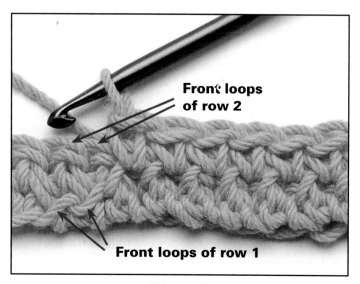

Front loops of row 2

Front loops of row 1

Photo C

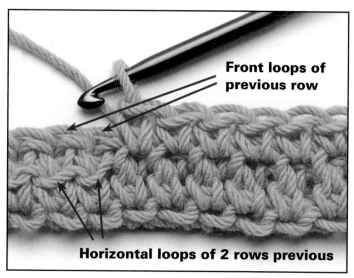

Front loops of previous row

Horizontal loops of 2 rows previous

Photo D

In project instructions, this is written (sc tog front lp from 2 rows previous and front lp from previous row) across, turn.

Row 4: Ch 1; *insert hook from bottom to top under front lp of sc 2 rows previous (front lps form a horizontal row), insert hook from bottom to top under front lp of sc in previous row, yo, draw through 2 front lps, yo and draw through 2 lps on hook; rep from * across, turn.

Rep row 4 for desired length.

In project instructions, this is written (sc tog front lp from 2 rows previous and front lp from previous row) or work in waffle weave pattern.

Last Row (Bind Off): Ch 1, (sc to front lp from 2 rows previous and both front and back lps from previous row) across.

Fasten off.

Colorful Dishcloth

EASY

Size
About 9 x 9½ inches

Materials
Medium (worsted) weight crochet cotton, 2 oz variegated; ½ oz red.
Note: *Our photographed dishcloth was made with Elmore-Pisgah Peaches & Crème, Fiesta Ombre #175 and Red #95.*
Size I/9/5.5mm crochet hook or size needed to obtain gauge
Tapestry needle

4 MEDIUM

Gauge
13 waffle weave sts = 4 inches

Instructions

With variegated, ch 26.

Row 1: Sk first ch, sc in front lp of each rem ch, turn. *(25 sc)*

Row 2: Ch 1, (sc tog front lp of beg ch and row 1) across, turn.

Row 3: Ch 1, (sc tog front lp from 2 rows previous and front lp from previous row) across, turn.

Rows 4–37: Rep row 3.

Row 38: Ch 1, (sc tog front lp from 2 rows previous and both front and back lps from previous row) across.

Fasten off and weave in ends.

Edging

Hold piece with last row worked at top; join red in upper right-hand corner; ch 3 (counts as a dc), 4 dc in same sp; dc in next 24 sts, 5 dc in next corner; working along next side, dc in end of next 36 rows, 5 dc in next corner; working along next side, dc in next 24 sts, 5 dc in next corner; working along next side, dc in end of next 36 rows; join in 3rd ch of beg ch-3.

Fasten off and weave in ends.

EASY

Size

About 4 x 80 inches

Materials

Light (light sport) weight yarn, 5 oz (372 yds, 150g) variegated; 1½ oz (111 yds, 45g) lime green

Note: *Our photographed scarf was made with Red Heart TLC Baby, frolic #7958 and lime #7624.*

Size K/10½/6.5mm crochet hook or size needed to obtain gauge

Tapestry needle

Gauge

12 waffle weave sts = 4 inches

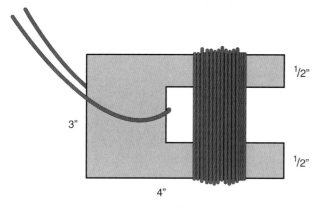

Fig. 1

Cut a piece of cardboard 3" x 4". Cut a U into one short side, leaving a minimum 1/2" all around. Cut a 2-foot length of yarn and place over base of U. Wrap yarn around cardboard 200 times, as shown in diagram, piling it upon itself.

Instructions

With variegated and leaving a 12-inch end, ch 13.

Row 1: Sk first ch, sc in front lp of each rem ch, turn. *(12 sc)*

Row 2: Ch 1, (sc tog front lp of beg ch and row 1) across, turn.

Row 3: Ch 1, (sc tog front lp from 2 rows previous and front lp from previous row) across, turn.

Rep row 3 until about 3 feet of yarn remains.

Last Row: Ch 1, (sc tog front lp from 2 rows previous and both front and back lps from previous row) across.

Fasten off.

Pompon (make 2)

Cut a piece of cardboard 3 x 4 inches. Cut a U into one short side leaving ½ inch sides. Cut a 24-inch length of lime green yarn and place over base of U. Referring to diagram, wrap lime green yarn around cardboard 200 times, piling it upon itself. Tie yarn strand at base of U tightly around center of wraps. Cut wraps apart along edges of cardboard. Trim pompon to shape.

Finishing

With tapestry needle, weave beg yarn end in and out of bottom lps of beg ch. Pull tight to gather and knot to secure. Rep on opposite end, weaving yarn end in and out of top lps of last row. Sew 1 pompon to each end of scarf.

Persimmon Placemat

EASY

Size

18 x 11 inches

Materials

Medium (worsted) weight crochet cotton, 4 oz variegated; 2½ oz persimmon

Note: *Our photographed place mat was made with Elmore-Pisgah Peaches & Crème, rainbow ombre #156 and persimmon #33.*

Size J/10/6mm crochet hook or size needed to obtain gauge

Tapestry needle

4

MEDIUM

Gauge

12 waffle weave sts = 4 inches

Instructions

With persimmon, ch 35.

Row 1: Sk first ch, sc in front lp of each rem ch, turn. *(34 sc)*

Row 2: Ch 1, (sc tog front lp of beg ch and row 1) across, turn.

Row 3: Ch 1, (sc tog front lp from 2 rows previous and front lp from previous row) across, turn.

Rows 4–13: Rep row 3.

Row 14: Ch 1, (sc tog front lp from 2 rows previous and front lp from previous row) across to last st; insert hook under 2 front lps of last st, yo, draw through, drop persimmon, pick up variegated and complete sc, turn. Fasten off persimmon.

Rows 15–59: Rep row 3.

Row 60: Ch 1, (sc tog front lp from 2 rows previous and front lp from previous row) across to last st; insert hook under 2 front lps of last st, yo, draw through, drop variegated, pick up persimmon and complete sc, turn. Fasten off variegated.

Rows 61–72: Rep row 3.

Row 73 (Bind Off): Ch 1, (sc tog front lp from 2 rows previous and both front and back lps from previous row) across.

Fasten off and weave in all ends.

Sweet-As-Candy Baby Afghan

EASY

Size

About 34 x 39 inches

Materials

Fine (sport) weight yarn, 8¾ oz (665 yds, 262g)
light purple; 7 oz (532 yds, 210g) each pink
and variegated

Note: *Our photographed baby afghan was
made with Patons Astra, pale lavender #02936, bright
pink #02845 and cotton candy variegated #02948.*

Size K/101/2/6.5mm crochet hook or size needed to
obtain gauge

Size G/6/4mm crochet hook

Tapestry needle

Gauge

With size K hook, 11 sts = 4 inches

Instructions

With K hook and light purple, ch 91 loosely.

Row 1: Sk first ch, sc in front lp of each rem ch, turn.
(90 sc)

Row 2: Ch 1, (sc tog front lp of beg ch and row 1)
across, turn.

Row 13: Ch 1, (sc tog front lp from 2 rows previous and
front lp from previous row) across to last st; insert hook
under 2 front lps of last st, yo, draw through, drop light
purple, pick up pink and complete sc, turn. Carry light
purple up side of work.

Row 4: Ch 1, (sc tog front lp from 2 rows previous and
front lp from previous row) across, turn.

Rows 5–152: Rep rows 3 and 4, changing colors every
2 rows in following sequence:

2 rows variegated

2 rows light purple

2 rows pink

Row 153 (Bind Off): With light purple, ch 1, (sc tog
front lp from 2 rows previous and both front and back
lps from previous row) across. Do not fasten off. Change
to G hook.

Border

Rnd 1: Working tightly, ch 1, 3 sc in corner sp; working
along next side in ends of rows, sc in each row to next
corner; 3 sc in corner sp; working across next side, *sc
in first st, 2 sc in next st; rep from * to next corner; 3 sc
in corner sp; working across next side in ends of rows
and working over carried yarns, sc in each row to next
corner; 3 sc in corner sp; working across row 153, *sc
in next 2 sc, sc in next post; rep from * to first sc; join in
first sc.

Rnd 2: Ch 1, sc in same sc; *3 sc in next sc; sc in each
sc to 2nd sc of next corner; rep from * twice more; 3 sc
in next sc; sc in each sc to first sc; join in first sc.

Rnd 3: Ch 1, sc in same sc and in next sc; *3 sc in next
sc; sc in each sc to 2nd sc of next corner; rep from *
twice more; 3 sc in next sc; sc in each sc to first sc; join
in first sc.

Rnd 4: Ch 1, sc in same sc and in next 2 sc; *4 sc in next
sc; sc in each sc to 2nd sc of next corner; rep from *
twice more; 4 sc in next sc; sc in each sc to first sc; join
in first sc.

Fasten off and weave in all ends.

Good Morning Sunshine Afghan

EASY

Size

About 42 x 58 inches

Materials

Fine (sport) weight yarn, 30 oz (3000 yds, 840g) yellow

Super Bulky (super chunky) yarn, 13½ oz (336 yds, 381g) variegated

Note: *Our photographed afghan was made with Red Heart Sport, yellow #230 and Red Heart Grande, wow #2937.*

Size P/15mm crochet hook or size needed to obtain gauge

Size I/9/5.5mm crochet hook

Size G/6/4mm crochet hook

Tapestry needle

Tape measure

Large paper clip

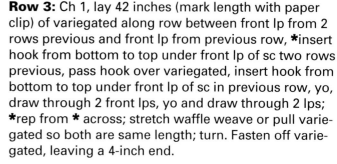

Gauge

With size P hook, 9 waffle weave sts = 4 inches

Instructions

With P hook and yellow, ch 101.

Row 1: Sk first ch, sc in front lp of each rem ch, turn. *(100 sc)*

Row 2: Ch 1, (sc tog front lp of beg ch and row 1) across, turn.

Row 3: Ch 1, lay 42 inches (mark length with paper clip) of variegated along row between front lp from 2 rows previous and front lp from previous row, *insert hook from bottom to top under front lp of sc two rows previous, pass hook over variegated, insert hook from bottom to top under front lp of sc in previous row, yo, draw through 2 front lps, yo and draw through 2 lps; *rep from * across; stretch waffle weave or pull variegated so both are same length; turn. Fasten off variegated, leaving a 4-inch end.

Note: *Work first few sts of next row over end.*

Rows 4–225: Rep row 3. At end of last row, change to I hook.

Row 226 (Bind Off): Ch 1, (sc tog front lp from 2 rows previous and both front and back lps from previous row) across. Do not turn. Change to G hook.

Edging

Note: *Edging is worked in continuous rnds. Do not join; mark beg of rnds.*

Rnd 1: 3 sc in end of row 225; working across side in ends of rows 224–2, sc in each row, working over yellow and through bend of variegated; 3 sc in end of row 1; working across next side, *sc in next post, sc in next 2 sts; rep from * across; working across next side in ends of rows, 3 sc in end of row 1; in end of rows 2–225, sc in each row, working over yellow and through bend of variegated; 3 sc in end of row 226; working across top, *sc in next 2 sc, sc in next post; rep from * across to first sc. Do not join.

Rnd 2: Sc in next sc; *3 sc in next sc; sc in each sc to 2nd sc of next corner; rep from * twice more; 3 sc in 2nd sc; sc in each sc to first sc.

Rnd 3: *Sc in each sc to 2nd sc of next corner; 3 sc in 2nd sc; rep from * 3 times more; sc in each sc to first sc.

Rnds 4–8: Rep rnd 3. At end of last rnd, join in first sc.

Fasten off and weave in all ends.

Good Morning Sunshine Pillow

EASY

Size

About 14 x 14 inches

Materials

Fine (sport) weight yarn, 7½ oz (750 yds, 210g) yellow

Super Bulky (super chunky) yarn, ½ oz (13 yds, 28g) variegated

3 LIGHT

6 SUPER BULKY

Note: *Our photographed afghan was made with Red Heart Sport, yellow #230 and Red Heart Grande, wow #2937.*

Size P/15mm crochet hook or size needed to obtain gauge

Size I/9/5.5mm crochet hook

Size G/6/4mm crochet hook

Tapestry needle

Tape measure

Large paper clip

14-inch pillow form

Gauge

9 waffle weave sts = 4 inches

Instructions

Front

With P hook and yellow, ch 21.

Row 1 (RS): Sk first ch, sc in front lp of each rem ch, turn. (20 sc)

Row 2: Ch 1, (sc tog front lp of beg ch and row 1) across, turn.

Row 3: Ch 1, lay 9 inches (mark length with paper clip) of variegated along row between front lp from 2 rows previous and front lp from previous row, *insert hook from bottom to top under front lp of sc two rows previous, pass hook over variegated, insert hook from bottom to top under front lp of sc in previous row, yo, draw through 2 front lps, yo and draw through 2 lps; *rep from * across; stretch waffle weave or pull variegated so both are same length; turn. Fasten off variegated, leaving a 4-inch end.

Note: *Work first few sts of next row over end.*

Rows 4–37: Rep row 3. At end of last row, change to I hook.

Row 38 (Bind Off): Ch 1, (sc tog front lp from 2 rows previous and both front and back lps from previous row) across. Do not turn. Change to G hook.

Edging

Note: *Edging is worked in continuous rnds. Do not join; mark beg of each rnd.*

Rnd 1: 4 sc in end of row 38; working across side in ends of rows 37–2, sc in each row, working over yellow and through bend of variegated; 4 sc in end of row 1; working across next side, *sc in next post, sc in next 2 sts; rep from * across; working across next side in ends of rows, 4 sc in end of row 1; in end of rows 2–37, sc in each row, working over yellow and through bend of variegated; 4 sc in end of row 38; working across top, *sc in next 2 sc, sc in next post; rep from * across to first sc. Do not join.

Rnd 2: Sc in next 3 sc, 3 sc in next sc; sc in each sc to next corner; 3 sc in next sc; sc in next 3 sc; sc in each sc to next corner; sc in next 3 sc, 3 sc in next sc; sc in each sc to next corner; 3 sc in next sc, sc in next 3 sc; sc in each sc to first sc.

Rnd 3: *Sc in each sc to 2nd sc of next corner; 2 sc in 2nd sc; rep from * 3 times more; sc in each sc to first sc.

Rnds 4–9: Rep rnd 3. At end of last rnd; join in first sc.

Fasten off and weave in all ends.

Back

With G hook and yellow, ch 4; join to form a ring.

Rnd 1: Ch 2 (counts as a sc), 12 sc in ring, do not join.

Note: *Remainder of back is worked in continuous rnds. Do not join; mark beg of rnds.*

Rnd 2: *3 sc in next sc—corner made; sc in next 2 sc; rep from * 3 times more;

Rnd 3: Sc in next sc, 2 sc in next sc; *sc in each sc to 2nd sc of next corner; 2 sc in 2nd sc; rep from * twice more; sc in each sc to first sc.

Rnds 4–26: Rep rnd 3. At end of last rnd, join in first sc.

Fasten off and weave in ends.

Finishing

Hold front and back wrong sides tog, matching corners. With G hook, join yellow in upper right-hand corner; working through both thicknesses at same time sc in each sc across 3 sides; insert pillow form, sc in each sc to first sc; join in first sc.

Fasten off and weave in ends.

Abbreviations & Symbols

beg .... begin/beginning
bpdc .... back post double crochet
bpsc .... back post single crochet
bptr .... back post treble crochet
CC .... contrasting color
ch .... chain stitch
ch- .... refers to chain or space previously made (i.e. ch-1 space)
ch sp .... chain space
cl .... cluster
cm .... centimeter(s)
dc .... double crochet
dc dec .... double crochet 2 or more stitches together, as indicated
dec .... decrease/decreases/decreasing
dtr .... double treble crochet
fpdc .... front post double crochet
fpsc .... front post single crochet
fptr .... front post treble crochet
g .... grams
hdc .... half double crochet
hdc dec ... half double crochet 2 or more stitches together, as indicated
lp(s) .... loops(s)
MC .... main color
mm .... millimeter(s)
oz .... ounce(s)
pc .... popcorn
rem .... remain/remaining
rep .... repeat(s)
rnd(s) .... round(s)
RS .... right side
sc .... single crochet
sc dec .... single crochet 2 or more stitches together, as indicated
sk .... skip
sl st .... slip stitch
sp(s) .... space(s)

st(s) .... stitch(es)
tog .... together
tr .... treble crochet
trtr .... triple treble
WS .... wrong side
yd(s) .... yard(s)
yo .... yarn over

* An asterisk (or double asterisk **) is used to mark the beginning of a portion of instructions to be worked more than once; thus, "rep from * twice more" means after working the instructions once, repeat the instructions following the asterisk twice more (3 times in all).

[] Brackets are used to enclose instructions that should be worked the exact number of times specified immediately following the brackets, such as "[2 sc in next dc, sc in next dc] twice." They are also used to set off and clarify a group of stitches that are to be worked all into the same space or stitch, such as "in next corner sp work [2 dc, ch 1, 2 dc]."

[] Brackets and () parentheses are used to provide additional information to clarify instructions.

Join—join with a sl st unless otherwise specified.

The patterns in this book are written using United States terminology. Terms that have different English equivalents are noted below.

United States	English
single crochet (sc)	double crochet (dc)
double crochet (dc)	treble (tr)
treble crochet (tr)	double treble (dtr)
skip (sk)	miss
slip stit ch (sl st)	slip stitch (ss) or single crochet
gauge	tension
yarn over (yo)	yarn over hook (YOH)

Chain—ch:
YO, draw through lp on hook.

Single Crochet—sc:
Insert hook in st, yo and draw through, yo and draw through both lps on hook.

Reverse Single Crochet—Reverse sc:
Work from left to right, insert hook in sp or st indicated (a), draw lp through sp or st - 2 lps on hook (b); yo and draw through lps on hook.

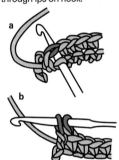

Half Double Crochet—hdc:
yo, insert hook in st, yo, draw through, yo and draw through all 3 lps on hook.

Double Crochet—dc:
yo, insert hook in st, yo, draw through, (yo and draw through 2 lps on hook) twice.

Triple Crochet—trc:
yo twice, insert hook in st, yo, draw through, (yo and draw through 2 lps on hook) 3 times.

Slip Stitch—sl st:
(a) Used for Joinings
Insert hook in indicated st, yo and draw through st and lp on hook.

(b) Used for Moving Yarn Over
Insert hook in st, yo draw through st and lp on hook.

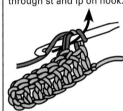

Front Loop—FL:
The front loop is the loop toward you at the top of the stitch.

Back Loop—BL:
The back loop is the loop away from you at the top of the stitch.

Post:
The post is the vertical part of the stitch.

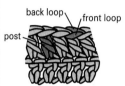

back loop front loop
post

Overcast Stitch is worked loosely to join crochet pieces.

Metric Chart

CROCHET HOOKS CONVERSION CHART

U.S.	1/B	2/C	3/D	4/E	5/F	6/G	8/H	9/I	10/J	10½/K	N
Continental-mm	2.25	2.75	3.25	3.5	3.75	4.25	5	5.5	6	6.5	9.0

Skill Levels

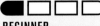

BEGINNER
Beginner projects for first-time crocheters using basic stitches. Minimal shaping.

EASY
Easy projects using basic stitches, repetitive stitch patterns, simple color changes and simple shaping and finishing.

INTERMEDIATE
Intermediate projects with a variety of stitches, mid-level shaping and finishing.

EXPERIENCED
Experienced projects using advanced techniques and stitches, detailed shaping and refined finishing.

Standard Yarn Weight System

Categories of yarn, gauge ranges, and recommended needle and hook sizes

Yarn Weight Symbol & Category Names	1 SUPER FINE	2 FINE	3 LIGHT	4 MEDIUM	5 BULKY	6 SUPER BULKY
Type of Yarns in Category	Sock, Fingering, Baby	Sport, Baby	DK, Light Worsted	Worsted, Afghan, Aran	Chunky, Craft, Rug	Bulky, Roving
Knit Gauge Range* in Stockinette Stitch to 4 inches	27–32 sts	23–26 sts	21–24 sts	16–20 sts	12–15 sts	6–11 sts
Recommended Needle in Metric Size Range	2.25–3.25 mm	3.25–3.75 mm	3.75–4.5 mm	4.5–5.5 mm	5.5–8 mm	8 mm and larger
Recommended Needle U.S. Size Range	1 to 3	3 to 5	5 to 7	7 to 9	9 to 11	11 and larger
Crochet Gauge* Ranges in Single Crochet to 4 inch	21–32 sts	16–20 sts	12–17 sts	11–14 sts	8–11 sts	5–9 sts
Recommended Hook in Metric Size Range	2.25–3.5 mm	3.5–4.5 mm	4.5–5.5 mm	5.5–6.5 mm	6.5–9 mm	9 mm and larger
Recommended Hook U.S. Size Range	B1–E4	E4–7	7–I9	I-9–K-10½	K-10½–M-13	M-13 and larger

* GUIDLINES ONLY: The above reflect the most commonly used gauges and needle or hook sizes for specific yarn categories.

American School of Needlework ®
excellence in instruction

DRG Publishing
306 East Parr Road
Berne, IN 46711
©2005 American School of Needlework
TOLL-FREE ORDER LINE or to request a free catalog (800) 582-6643
Customer Service (800) 282-6643, Fax (800) 882-6643

Visit AnniesAttic.com.

Customer Service (800) 282-6643, **fax** (800) 882-6643